A Celebration of Love

A Celebration of Love

Thoughts & Ideas for the Romantic at Heart

Compiled and Illustrated by
LESLEY BOSTON

BANTAM BOOKS
SYDNEY • AUCKLAND • TORONTO • NEW YORK • LONDON

A CELEBRATION OF LOVE

A BANTAM BOOK

Printing History
Bantam edition published 1990

Copyright © Bow Press

All rights reserved. No part of this publication may be reproduced, stored in a retrieval system, or transmitted in any form, or by any means, electronic, mechanical, photocopying, recording or otherwise, without the prior permission of the publishers.

National Library of Australia
Cataloguing-in-Publication entry

A Celebration of Love: Thoughts and ideas for the romantic at heart.
ISBN 0 947189 84 X
1. Love — Miscellanea. 2. Love — Literary Collections.
I. Boston, Lesley.
306.7

Bantam Books are published in Australia by
Transworld Publishers (Australia) Pty Limited
15-23 Helles Ave, Moorebank, NSW 2150 and in
New Zealand by Transworld Publishers (NZ) Limited
Cnr Moselle and Waipareira Aves, Henderson Auckland.

The author and the publishers wish to thank Denise Greig for her Herbal Love Bath recipe taken from her book *Potpourri and Perfumery from Australian Gardens.*

Typeset by Excel Imaging Pty Ltd, Sydney
Produced by Mandarin Offset in Hong Kong

Designed by Cate Hickson
Calligraphy by Christina Beaumont

Produced in association with Bow Press, 208 Victoria Road, Drummoyne NSW 2047

Introduction

Just a hint of romance can be enough to send hearts a-flutter. When captured by its charms, all things beautiful remind us of love. We woo our loved ones with special gifts, following traditions of courtship that are packed with meaning.

Romantic love burns in our hearts today as strongly as it ever did. Love transcends time and cultures — it is a universal emotion, a universal language. Poets, songwriters, novelists and philosophers have exalted the joys of love in a multitude of ways. This collection, small enough to carry close to your heart, captures some of those precious moments.

Darling Lily

Valentines

Valentines originally were a piece of folded paper bearing the name of a boy or girl, drawn by lot at parties on the eve of St Valentine's Day (14 February). The one named on the slip of paper was to be the sweetheart of the drawer for the year.

Other traditions associated with St Valentine's Day relate to the first young man or woman one chances to meet on St Valentine's Day. The custom was to kiss this 'first-met' and thus they were your special valentine for the year.

The fancy Victorian valentine card was beflowered and befilled with ribbons and paper lace. It bore printed or written verses couching a love greeting or proposal.

The rose is red, the violet's blue
The honey's sweet, and so are you.
Thou art my love and I am thine;
I drew thee to my Valentine:
The lot was cast and then I drew,
And fortune said it shou'd be you.
From GAMMER GURTIN'S GARLAND

Valentine Cake

Ingredients

Cake Mixture
75 g (3 oz) castor sugar
3 eggs
75 g (3 oz) plain flour
½ teaspoon baking powder

Icing
250 g (8 oz) icing sugar, sifted
3 tablespoons boiling water
red food colouring

Filling
Raspberry jam
125 g (4oz) ground almonds
70 g (2 oz) castor sugar
70 g (2 oz) icing sugar
1 egg yolk
almond essence
1 teaspoon kirsch

Decoration
Pink and red coated chocolate buttons

Method

Brush a 20 cm (8 in) heart-shaped cake tin with oil (alternatively use a round cake tin, and cut the cake into a heart shape when it is cooked). Line the base and sides with greaseproof paper and grease the paper.

Put the eggs and sugar in a bowl and stand it over hot water. Whisk until the mixture becomes thick, then remove the bowl from the heat and carry on whisking until cool. Fold in the sifted flour and baking powder.

Pour the mixture into the prepared tin and shake gently to level the top. Bake at 180° C, Gas mark 4 for 30-35 minutes. Leave to cool completely before removing from the tin.

Brush the top of the cake with raspberry jam. Mix the almonds and both sugars together. Beat the egg yolk with a few drops of almond essence and the kirsch. Stir into the almond mixture and mix to a paste. Roll out the almond paste to a size slightly larger than the cake. place the paste on the cake and cut around the edges so that it covers the top.

Mix the icing sugar with enough boiling water so that the icing thickly coats the back of the spoon. Add a drop of red food colouring to tint the icing pink. Place the cake on a wire rack over a plate. using a large spoon, pour the icing over. When the icing has stopped falling, carefully transfer the cake to a silver cake board. Decorate with coated chocolate buttons and leave to set.

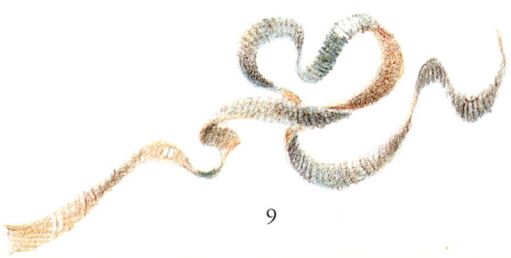

Say it with Flowers

Acacia, yellow — secret love
Amaranth (Golbe) — unfading love
Ambrosia — love returned
Bluebell — constancy
Carnation, pink — woman's love
Catchfly, red — youthful love
Chrysanthemum, red — I love you
Coreopsis, Arkansa — love at first sight
Dandelion — love's oracle
Double Pink, red — love, pure and ardent
Forget-me-not — true love
Honey Flower — sweet and secret love
Lemon blossoms — fidelity in love
Lilac, purple — first emotions of love

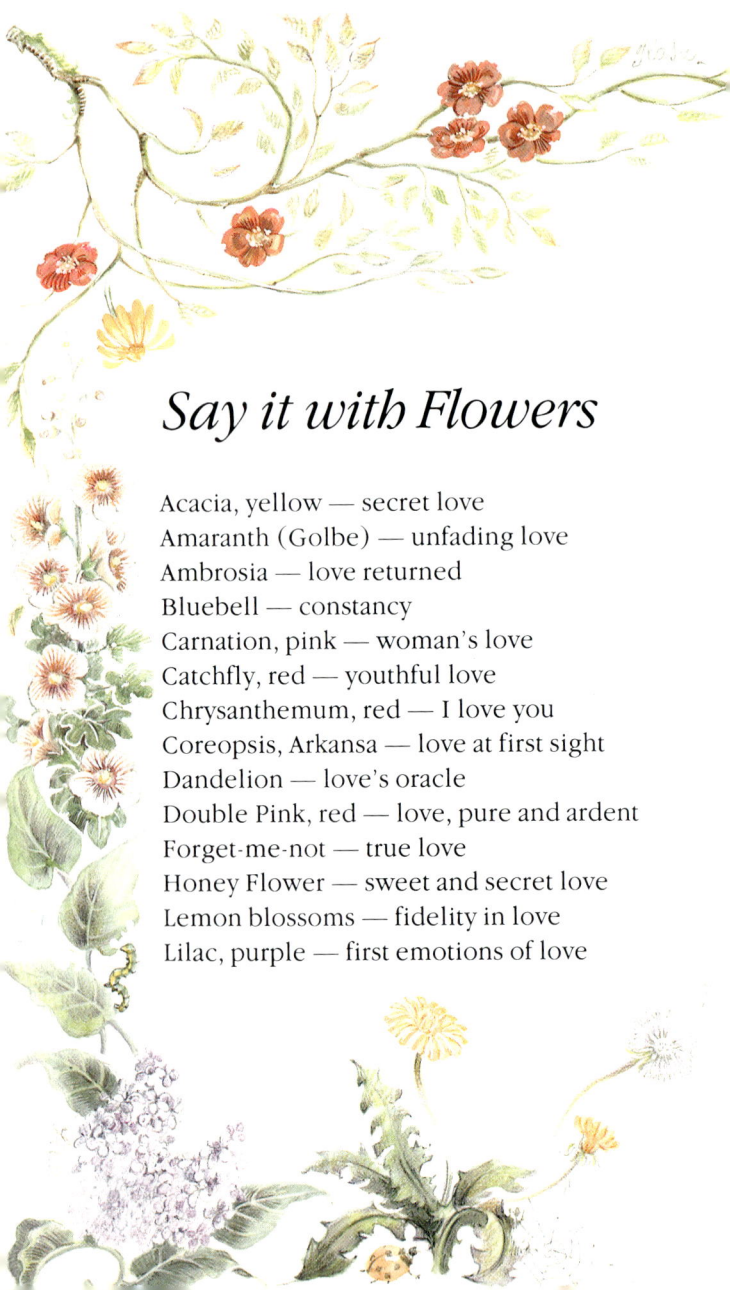

Mellow Syrian — consumed by love
Motherwort — concealed love
Myrtle — love
Rose — love
Rose, Austrian — thou art all that is lovely
Rose, Bridal — happy love
Rose, Cabbage — ambassador of love
Rose, Campion — only you deserve my love
Rose, Carolina — love is dangerous
Rose, Maiden Blush — if you love me, you will find it out
Rosebud, Moss — confessions of love
Strawberry Tree — esteem and love
Tulip, red — declaration of love

Songs

If music be the food of love, play on.
Shakespeare

Are you going to Scarborough Fair?
Parsley, sage, rosemary and thyme,
Remember me to one who lives there,
She once was a truelove of mine.

Tell her to find me an acre of land
Parsley, sage, rosemary and thyme,
Between the salt water, and the sea strand,
Then she'll be a truelove of mine.

Tell her to make me a candlewick shirt
Parsley, sage, rosemary and thyme,
Without any seams nor needlework,
Then she'll be a truelove of mine.

Frankie and Johnny were lovers
O Lordy, how they could love.
Swore to be true to each other,
True as the stars above...
Anon

All You Need is Love
John Lennon and Paul McCartney

Let's Do It; Let's Fall in Love
Cole Porter, PARIS

Love and marriage, love and marriage
Go together like a horse and carriage
Harry Cahn, OUR TOWN

Bobby Shafter's gone to sea,
Silver buckles on his knee,
He'll come back and marry me,
Bonny Bobby Shafter.

Bobby Shafter's tall and fair,
Combing down his golden hair,
He's my love for ere and ere,
Bonny Bobby Shafter.

Curly Locks, Curly Locks wilt thou be mine?
Thou shall not wash dishes, nor yet feed the
 swine,
But sit on a cushion, and sew a fine seam,
And feed upon strawberries, sugar and cream.

Lavender's blue dilly dilly,
Lavender's green,
When I am king dilly dilly,
You shall be queen.

Call up your men dilly dilly,
Set them to work,
Some to the plough dilly dilly
Some to the fork.

Some to cut hay dilly dilly,
Some to cut corn,
While you and I dilly dilly,
Keep ourselves warm.

Love Games

Eating cherries? How many stones are there on your plate when you have finished? Count them using the following words to determine the kind of man you will marry:

Tinker, tailor, soldier, sailor, richman, poorman, beggarman, thief, doctor, lawyer, merchant, chief.

Does your sweetheart love you?

Pull the petals off a daisy until they are all gone, reciting the following words:

He/she loves me
He/she loves me not
He/she loves me
He/she loves me not...etc.

Peel an apple or an orange so that the peel comes off in one whole spiral strip. Then throw the peel over your shoulder. It will land in the shape of a letter and this is the initial of the one you will marry.

Forget-me-not

Lily of the valley

If you have white flecks in your fingernails, check to see if there are any on the fourth finger (the one next to the little finger). On your left hand, this indicates a sweetheart in the future, and on your right hand a sweetheart in the past. Each finger represents a different fortune: the rhyme you use to remember what each one means starts at the thumb, and goes:

a friend, a present, a foe, a sweetheart, a journey to go.

When blowing out candles on a birthday cake, the number of puffs it takes equals the number of girlfriends/boyfriends you have.

To see how compatible you are with your loved one, write out both of your names in full. Then cross out all the letters that are common to both names. If one name has the letter 'l' three times, and the other has it only two times, cross out only two 'l's in each name. You will be left with a certain number of letters for each name. Count these up using the following words to determine your attitudes to each other:

love, hate, marriage, adore, love, hate, marriage, adore, etc.

Sweetheart Cocktail

30ml (1 fl oz) strawberry liqueur
champagne
2-3 strawberries
½ scoop ice

Blend strawberry liqueur with strawberries and ice. Pour into a flute glass and top up with champagne. Garnish with a heart-shaped strawberry.

LOVE POTIONS

Mandrake was used to make love potions. Its fruit would make the one drinking the potion fall in love with the one who offered it.

LOVING CUP

This is a cup with several handles designed to be passed around a circle of friends. All night long they drink to love.

Superstitions

Throwing a loved one's article of clothing into a fire is said to cause an absent lover to burn with desire.

In ancient Denmark, lovers pledged fidelity by sprinkling blood into the footprint of each other.

In an old Slavic tradition, the earth of a sweetheart's footprint was dug up and a marigold planted in it. The marigold flourished until either one or the other of the sweetheart's love failed.

In Sweden on Midsummer's Night (24 June), young girls go into the meadow and pick seven different flowers. They make these into a bouquet and put them under their pillow. They are then supposed to dream about their future husband.

Love is like the rose: so sweet that one always
tries to gather it in spite of the thorns.
Anon

There's nothing half so sweet in life
As love's young dream.
Thomas Moore, LOVE'S YOUNG DREAM

Is there on earth a space so dear
As that within the blessed sphere
Two loving arms entwine?
Thomas Moore, TO FANNY

Love is, above all, the gift of oneself.
Jean Anouilh, ARDÈLE

I ne'er was struck before that hour
With love so sudden and so sweet.
Her face it bloomed like a sweet flower
And stole my heart away complete.
My face turned pale as deadly pale,
My legs refused to walk away,
And when she looked 'what could I ail?'
My life and all seemed turned to clay.

And then my blood rushed to my face
And took my sight away.
The trees and bushes round the place
Seemed midnight at noonday.
I could not see a single thing,
Words from my eyes did start;
They spoke as chords do from the string
And blood burnt round my heart

Are flowers the winter's choice?
Is love's bed always snow?
She seemed to hear my silent voice
And love's appeal to know.
I never saw so sweet a face
As that I stood before:
My heart has left its dwelling-place
And can return no more.
John Clare, FIRST LOVE, 1793-1864

Courtly Love

The Gothic period was a romantic time. From the twelfth to the fifteenth centuries, Europeans had the notion of an idealised love. The rich usually married for convenience, to secure wealth and property, and love did not enter into the arrangement. Instead there was a tradition of courtly love, whereby knights would dedicate sometimes a lifetime to performing acts of bravery for their fair lady (who was often married). No sacrifice was too great.

The knights of King Arthur's round table were chivalrous romantics, and there were many stories told of their adventures. The troubadours were travelling musicians in France who told of dream-like romances. Long stories about courtly love told in prose or verse became popular, in particular one called the *Roman de la Rose*. Famous authors include Chretien de Troyes and Malory.

'Tis love, like the sun, that gives light to the
  year,
The sweetest of blessings that life can give;
Our pleasures it brightens, drives sorrow away,
Gives joy to the night, and enlivens the day.
Edward Moore

Love like air is widely given;
Power nor chance can these restrain;
Truest, noblest gifts of heaven!
Only purest in the plain.
William Shenstone

Chocolate Dreams

Ingredients

300 g (12 oz) milk chocolate
1 cup finely chopped almonds
¾ cup sweetened condensed milk
1 teaspoon rum
200 g (8 oz) dark chocolate for coating

Method

Break the milk chocolate into a bowl, and place over a pan of hot water. When the chocolate has melted, add the almonds, condensed milk and rum and beat with a wooden spoon until the mixture is completely blended and slightly thickened. Then leave it to cool in the refrigerator for at least 2 hours, preferably overnight.

Roll the mixture into little balls. Melt the dark chocolate in a bowl over hot water, and coat the the chocolate dreams by dipping them in the melted chocolate. Place them on a sheet of greaseproof paper to set.

Romantic Novels

Gone with the Wind, Margaret Mitchell
Jane Eyre, Charlotte Brontë
Rebecca, Daphne du Maurier
Love Story, Erich Segal
Pride and Prejudice, Jane Austen
Persuasion, Jane Austen
Mansfield Park, Jane Austen
Dr Zhivago, Boris Pasternak
Under the Greenwood Tree, Thomas Hardy
I Capture the Castle, Dodie Smith
Love in the Time of Cholera, Gabriel Garcia
   Marquez
The Go Between, L.P. Hartley
Wuthering Heights, Emily Brontë

and anything written by Georgette Heyer and
Barbara Cartland.

Love is Universal

PORTUGUESE

Amor não tem lei
Love has no law

GERMAN

Liebe wintert nicht
Tieck
Love knows no winter

ITALIAN

Amor nel nostro petto
E un volontario affetto;
Nè mai forza o rigore
Può limitar la liberta del core.
Metastasio

*Love is a feeling that comes into our hearts
of our own choice;
For neither force nor harshness
can limit the heart's freedom.*

Amor no conosce travaglio
Love never tires

Amor tutti fa uguali
Love makes all men equal

FRENCH

L'amour est le plus matinal de nos sentiments
Fontinelle
Love is the earliest of our feelings

L'amour est une pure rosée qui descend du ciel dans notre cœur, quand il plaît à Dieu.
Love is a pure dew which drops from heaven into our heart, when God wills.

L'amour est un plaisir qui tormente,
mais ce tourment fait plaisir.
Scribe
Love is a pleasure that teases,
but this teasing is pleasing.

LATIN

Amor gignit amorem
Love begets love

Amor magnus doctor est
St Augustine
Love is a great teacher

Amor timere neminem verus potest
Seneca
True love can fear no one

Amor vincit omnia
Love conquers all

Iris —
"HINDU MAGIC"

'Whether love be natural or no,' replied my friend, gravely, 'it contributes to the happiness of every society into which it is introduced. All our pleasures are short, and can only charm at intervals: love is a method of protracting our greatest pleasure; and surely that gamester who plays the greatest stake to the best advantage will, at the end of life, rise victorious.'
Goldsmith, CITIZEN OF THE WORLD CXVI

Oh, how beautiful it is to love! Even thou that sneerest and laughest in cold indifference or scorn if others are near thee, — thou, too, must acknowledge its truth when thou art alone, and confess that a foolish world is prone to laugh in public at what in private it reveres as one of the highest impulses of our nature; namely, love.
Longfellow

Love, as is told by the seers of old,
comes as a butterfly tipped with gold,
Fluters and flies in sunlit skies,
Weaving round hearts that were one time cold.
Swinburne, SONG

Oysters are considered to be an aphrodisiac. Of course you can eat them chilled with just a squeeze of lemon juice, but if you prefer to cook a sumptuous dish to whet your lover's appetite, here is a recipe for...

Hot Lovers' Oysters

Ingredients

12 oysters in the half shell
coarse sea salt
25 g (1 oz) butter
salt
pinch of sugar

squeeze of lemon juice
170 ml (6 fl oz) double cream
1 egg yolk
pinch of curry powder

Method

Steam the oysters in their shells for one minute, or until plump. Strain the juices from the oysters through a fine sieve into a small pan. Add the butter, sugar, curry powder, lemon juice and a pinch of salt, and bring to the boil. Beat the cream with the egg yolk in a bowl. Pour in the boiling flavoured oyster juices stirring briskly.

Arrange the oysters in their shells on a bed of coarse sea salt in a heatproof dish. This will keep them level. Fill the shells with the sauce, making sure each oyster is thoroughly coated. Place the dish under a hot grill for a minute or so to glaze. Serve immediately in a candle-lit setting.

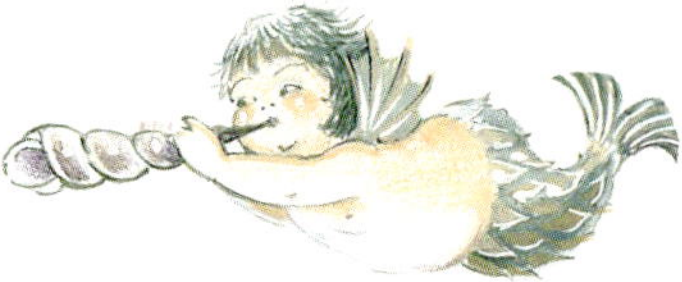

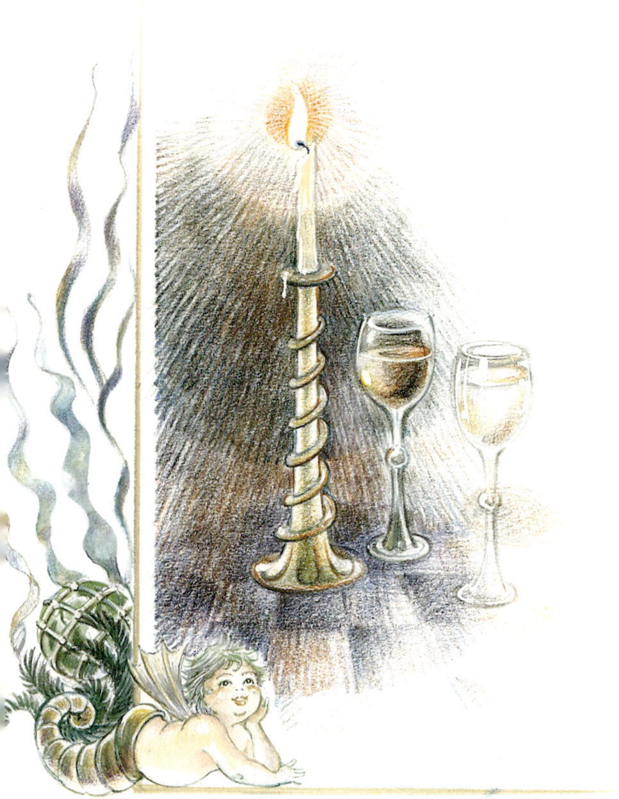

Passionfruit

PASSIFLORA CAERULEA

Famous lovers

Abélard and Hélöise
Adam and Eve
Beauty and the Beast
Bonnie and Clyde
Cleopatra and Mark Antony
Cinderella and the Prince
Cupid and Psyche
Darby and Joan
Eros and Psyche
Heathcliff and Cathy
Jack and Jill
John Lennon and Yoko Ono
Kind Edward and Mrs Simpson
Lancelot and Guinevere
Napoleon and Josephine
Punch and Judy
Queen Victoria and Prince Albert
Richard Burton and Elizabeth Taylor
Robin Hood and Maid Marian
Romeo and Juliet
Samson and Delilah
Tristan and Isolde
Troilus and Cressida
Ying and Yang
Zeus and Alcmene

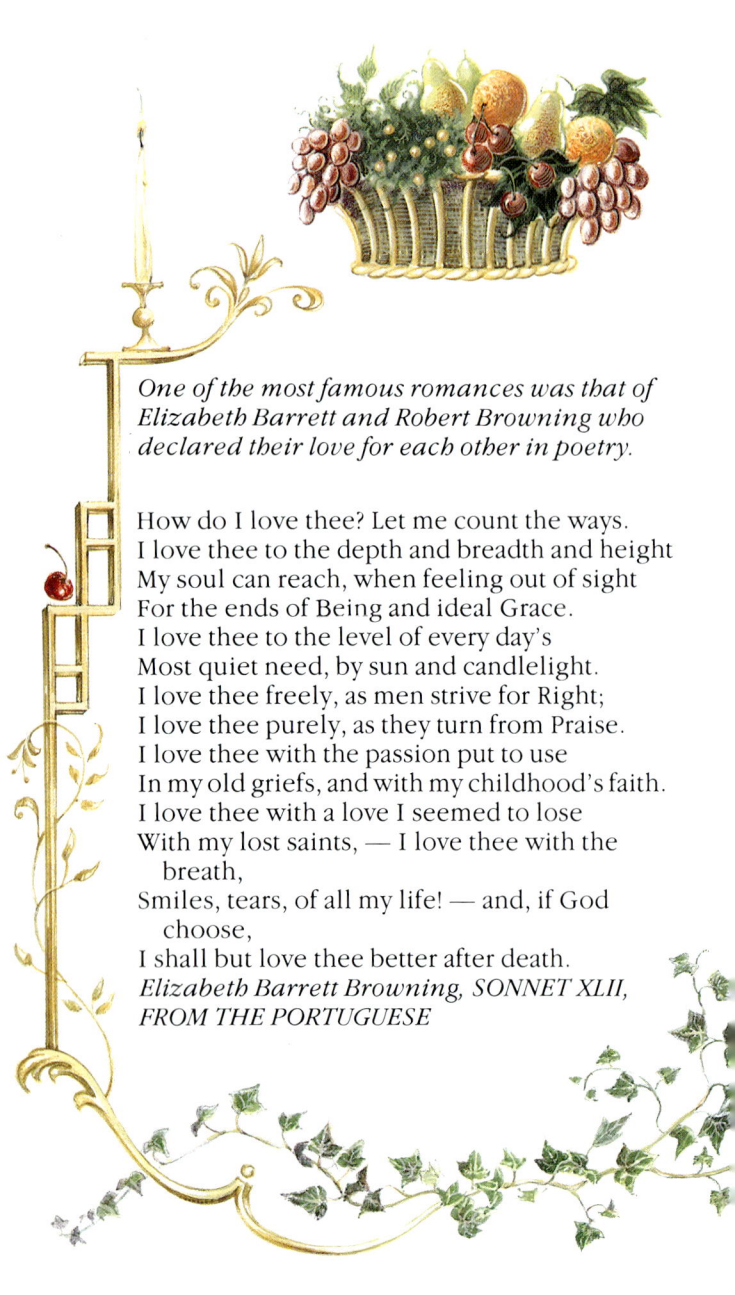

One of the most famous romances was that of Elizabeth Barrett and Robert Browning who declared their love for each other in poetry.

How do I love thee? Let me count the ways.
I love thee to the depth and breadth and height
My soul can reach, when feeling out of sight
For the ends of Being and ideal Grace.
I love thee to the level of every day's
Most quiet need, by sun and candlelight.
I love thee freely, as men strive for Right;
I love thee purely, as they turn from Praise.
I love thee with the passion put to use
In my old griefs, and with my childhood's faith.
I love thee with a love I seemed to lose
With my lost saints, — I love thee with the breath,
Smiles, tears, of all my life! — and, if God choose,
I shall but love thee better after death.
Elizabeth Barrett Browning, SONNET XLII, FROM THE PORTUGUESE

So, the year's done with
(Love me for ever!)
All March begun with,
April's endeavour;
May-wreaths that bound me
June needs must sever;
Now snows fall round me,
Quenching June's fever-
(Love me for ever!)
Robert Browning, LOVE, 1812-1889

What's the earth
With all its art, verse, music, worth —
Compared with love, found, gained, and kept
Robert Browning, DIS ALITER VISUM

Love is best!
Robert Browning, LOVE AMONG THE RUINS

Love Charms

Gems, rings and other jewels are worn or used to bring good fortune in love.

The exchange of wedding rings grew out of the practice of exchanging love charms as a pledge of love or as a guarantee to the continuance of love. Lovers sometimes exchange bits of hair, clothing, rings, and even blood.

A common charm in various parts of the world is made by melting the image of a loved one; as the image melts coldness supposedly melts into love.

Pink Wedding Bush

She who hath felt a real pain
By Cupid's dart,
Finds that all absence is in vain
To cure her heart.
Though from my lover cast
Far as from Pole to Pole,
Still the pure flame must last,
For love is of the Soul.
John Gay, 1685-1782

The aspects which procure love are not gazings, but sudden glances and dartings of the eye.
Lord Bacon

No cord or cable can draw so forcibly, or bind so fast, as love can do with only a single thread.
Lord Bacon

The ring, so worn as you behold,
So thin, so pale, is yet of gold.
The passion such it was to prove:
Worn with life's care, love yet was love.
George Crabbe, 1754-1832

The affirmation of one's own life, happiness, growth, freedom is rooted in one's capacity to love.
Erich Fromm, THE ART OF LOVING

Beloved, let us love one another: for love is of God; and every one that loveth is born of God and knoweth God.
He that loveth not knoweth not God; for God is love.
I. John, iv. 7,8.

Gods of Love

EROS — THE GREEK GOD OF LOVE

Eros was a beautiful and mischievous youth renowned for driving chariots, hunting, rowing and shooting love arrows.

In art, he is generally shown as a chubby winged boy bearing bow and quiver, sometimes a torch. He is depicted riding a dolphin, an eagle, a lion, or seated in a chariot drawn by wild boars or stags, emblematic of the power of love as the subduer of all nature including wild animals.

APHRODITE — THE GREEK GODDESS OF BEAUTY AND LOVE — AND VENUS — THE ROMAN GODDESS OF LOVE

Aphrodite was fabled to have been born of sea foam and, standing on a scallop shell, she was washed ashore. Botticelli's *Birth of Venus* is an exact icon.

CUPID — THE ROMAN GOD OF FIRST BORN LOVE

Like Eros, Cupid is usually depicted as a winged unaging boy, naked but armed with a bow and arrow. Sometimes he is blindfoleded to indicate he strikes indiscriminately. His broken bow signifies love conquered, his golden arrow virtuous love, and his leaden arrow sensual passion.

Herbal Love Bath

Ingredients

1 cup lavender
1 cup rosemary
1 cup rose petals
1/2 cup lovage
1/2 cup lemon verbena leaves
1 tablespoon each thyme, mint, sage, marjoram, and orrisroot powder

Method

Mix all ingredients thoroughly and keep in a tightly lidded container. To use, pack 1/4 cup in a muslin square and tie securely. Bring the bath ball to the boil in about 1 cup of water and let it stand for 10 minutes. Add to hot bath water and scrub yourself with the little love bath ball. Think romantic thoughts and luxuriate.

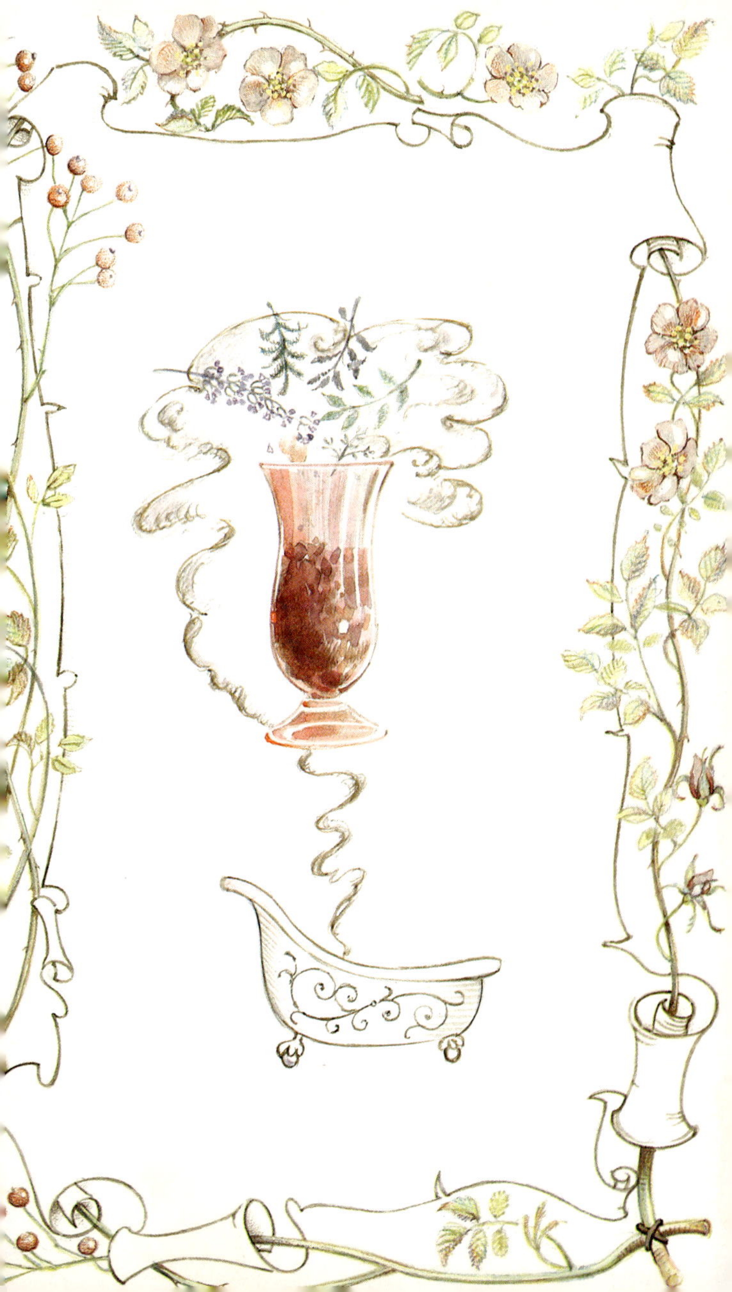

This is the miracle that happens every time to those who really love: the more they give, the more they possess of that precious nourishing love from which flowers and children have their strength and which could help all human beings if they would take it without doubting. . .
Rainer Maria Rilke

Love does not dominate; it cultivates
Goethe

'Tis better to have loved and lost,
Than never to have loved at all.
Tennyson, IN MEMORIAM

The consciousness of being loved softens the keenest pang, even at the moment of parting; yea, even the eternal farewell is robbed of half its bitterness when uttered in accents that breathe love to the last sight.
Addison

Morning Glory – "HEAVENLY BLUE"

Astrological Heart Mates

Here are some ideal matches that should lead to romantic fulfilment:

> Aries — Leo
> Aries — Sagittarius
> Taurus — Virgo
> Taurus — Capricorn
> Cancer — Scorpio
> Cancer — Pisces
> Leo — Sagittarius
> Virgo — Capricorn
> Libra — Gemini
> Libra — Aquarius
> Scorpio — Pisces
> Aquarius — Gemini

Moonflower Vine

Love Dances

In some parts of the world prospective lovers still perform ritual dances. The dances display the beauty and grace, energy and force, endurance and skill of courtship.

In the Fiji islands, the dance is performed in a seated position and celebrated with a sacred drink called ava.

In Java and Madagascar, the dance is carried out with the hands and arms exclusively.

In Tunisia the dance is one of the hair; all night long until they fall exhausted, marriageable girls move their head to the rhythm of a song, maintaining their hair in perpetual balance and sway.

Lunaria annua — Honesty

Honesty – LUNARIA

By love's delightful influence the attack of ill-humour is resisted, the violence of our passions abated, the bitter cup of affliction sweetened, all the injuries of the world alleviated, and the sweetest flowers plentifully strewed along the most thorny paths of life.
Zimmerman

Love is like a rose, the joy of all the earth,...
Love is like a lovely rose, the world's delight.
Christina Rosetti, HOPE

Lovely as Love
Byron

Love is better than spectacles to make everything seem great.
Sir P. Sidney

Foxglove

DIGITALIS PURPUREA

Symbols of Love

The colour crimson, doves, hearts, the image of a heart pierced by an arrow, lodestone, the colour red, roses.

Personified by: Cherubim, Cupid, Eros.

Deep love: symbolised by an amethyst or ruby

Divine love: symbolised by crimson colour, dianthus, flaming heart

Illicit love: symbolised by aconite

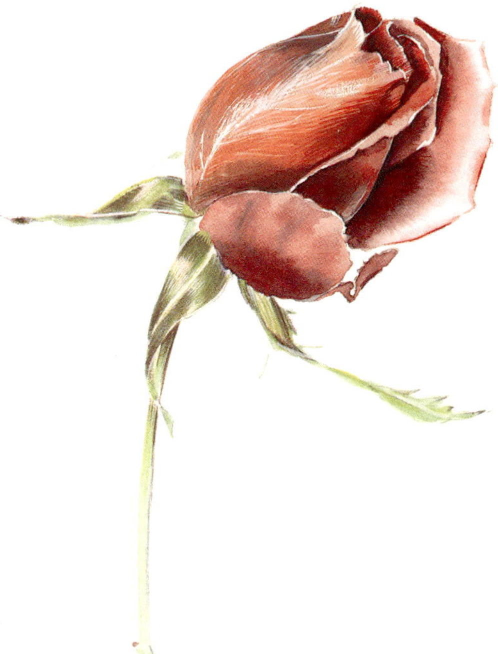

I love you *(English)*

Ich liebe Dich *(German)*

Je t'aime *(French)*

Te quiero *(Spanish)*

Ti amo *(Italian)*

Jag älskar dig *(Swedish)*

S'agapau *(Greek)*

Seretlek *(Hungarian)*

Ich ha dich gärn *(Swiss-German)*

Eu amo te *(Portuguese)*

Jeg elsker dig *(Danish)*

Mina rakastan sinna *(Finnish)*